KETO
Power Bowls

KETO
Power Bowls

Easy, Nutritious, Low-Carb, High-Fat Meals for Busy People

Faith Gorsky

Skyhorse Publishing

Skyhorse Publishing books may be purchased in bulk at special discounts for sales promotion, corporate gifts, fund-raising, or educational purposes. Special editions can also be created to specifications. For details, contact the Special Sales Department, Skyhorse Publishing, 307 West 36th Street, 11th Floor, New York, NY 10018 or info@skyhorsepublishing.com.

Skyhorse® and Skyhorse Publishing® are registered trademarks of Skyhorse Publishing, Inc.®, a Delaware corporation.

Visit our website at www.skyhorsepublishing.com.

10 9 8 7 6 5 4 3

Library of Congress Cataloging-in-Publication Data is available on file.
Library of Congress Control Number: 2020933028

Cover design by Erin Seaward-Hiatt
Cover photograph credit: Faith Gorsky
Interior photographs by Faith Gorsky

Print ISBN: 978-1-5107-5456-0
Ebook ISBN: 978-1-5107-5893-3

Printed in China

To my mom, Elizabeth,
who always made sure my siblings and I ate well-balanced meals
and sat down to family dinner every single night.

Table of Contents

KETO
Power Bowls

CHAPTER 1
What a Balanced Meal Looks Like on a Ketogenic Diet

Macronutrients in a Ketogenic Diet

When you're following a ketogenic diet and meal plan, the goal is to force your body to run on ketones instead of on carbohydrates. The way we achieve that is by lowering our carbohydrate intake, increasing our healthy fat intake, and eating a moderate amount of protein. Your personal health goals—whether it is to gain weight, lose weight, or maintain your current weight—will determine your macronutrient levels, meaning what percentage of fat, protein, and carbohydrates you need to consume in order to maintain a state of nutritional ketosis.

The factors that determine your macronutrient requirements are:

- Gender
- Age
- Height
- Weight
- Activity level
- Body fat percentage
- Health goals (i.e., to lose, maintain, or gain weight)

The easiest, most efficient way to figure out your macronutrient requirements is to use a macronutrient calculator. If you do a simple Google search, you can find a plethora of free calculators online from reputable brands. On my website, www.TheKetoQueens.com, I have an entire post dedicated to reviewing various macronutritient calculators called "Keto Macro Calculator Review."

As a general rule of thumb, the macronutrient percentages for a ketogenic diet are as follows:

- 60 to 75 percent of calories from fat
- 15 to 30 percent of calories from protein
- 5 to 10 percent of calories from carbohydrates

Once you know your body's macronutrient requirements, you can start meal planning and plugging in foods to see how they fit into your eating regimen.

What Does a Balanced Ketogenic Diet Look Like?

Something to remember is that you don't have to follow your specific macronutrient percentages at each and every single meal, but rather for your meal plan for the entire day. However, with that being said, it's often easier to stay on track with your macros if you at least generally follow the percentages for each macronutrient at most meals.

So, what does a balanced meal look like?

Contrary to popular belief, and the joke of so many memes that us keto-eaters only eat bacon, mayo, and heavy cream, the goal is to eat a variety of good quality fats, proteins, and low carbohydrate foods. We eat tons of low-carb vegetables and even some low-carb fruit!

And it gets even better. Not only are we not deprived of fresh produce, but we don't have to limit ourselves to the same old grilled meat + steamed vegetables + butter formula. (I mean, grilled steak with buttered broccoli is delicious, but it gets a little boring after a while, right?!) A well-balanced, keto-friendly meal doesn't have to be boring, and you should never feel deprived.

A balanced meal might consist of poached eggs (which provide protein and fat with minimal carbs) along with summer squash (the main source of carbohydrates in this meal) and turkey sausage (for protein) hash. Or it could be fish scampi (for protein) with garlic butter (the source of fat) zoodles (carbohydrates). Or, a balanced meal could come in the form of dessert! Maybe it's a low-carb high-fat strawberry shortcake, with shortcake that's made with a base of nut flour (providing protein, fat, and carbohydrates) and topped with a dollop of whipped cream (for fat).

The power bowl meals in this cookbook will provide a combination of healthy fat, protein, and carbohydrates that you can fit into your ketogenic meal plan.

CHAPTER 2

Power Bowl Components, Keto-Style

You'll have tons of options when you're putting together a low-carb high-fat power bowl meal to help you meet your macronutrient requirements and stay in ketosis. Here are a few ideas (this is by no means a comprehensive list because that would be an entire book in itself!), many of which you'll find recipes for in this cookbook, broken down by macronutrient type.

Note that many foods provide more than one macronutrient and could technically be classified into two or even all three categories. For example, eggs mainly provide protein and fat, but they also have a small amount of carbohydrates.

Healthy Fat Sources

- Nutritious oils, such as avocado, olive, and coconut
- Grass-fed butter, ghee, and dairy products, such as cheese and cream
- High-fat low-carb fruit, such as avocado (or guacamole!), olives, and coconut
- High-fat low-carb nuts, such as macadamia nuts, walnuts, pecans, Brazil nuts, hazelnuts, and almonds

- Homemade low-carb high-fat vinaigrettes or creamy dressings

Nutrient-Dense Proteins

- Grass-fed red meat
- Free-range poultry
- Wild-caught seafood
- Free-range eggs

Low-Carb Vegetable Bases

- Zucchini—for zucchini noodles, of course
- Cucumber (technically a fruit) —for cucumber noodles or salads
- Cauliflower—for cauliflower "rice" or as a pasta or potato simulation
- Spaghetti squash—to replace regular spaghetti noodles
- Leafy greens mix—as a bed for a variety of salads
- Slaw mix—as a bed for things like BBQ beef or as a condiment for things like chipotle lime fish
- Sautéed cabbage—when you want a warm base that somewhat simulates noodles

CHAPTER 3

Swapping Out Components to Create New Flavor Profiles

Keto power bowls are highly customizable! If there's a component of a power bowl that you don't like, you can simply swap it out for something you prefer. (Just be aware that changing ingredients will change the nutritional value.)

For example:

- Use Grilled Steak (p. 99) instead of chicken in Chicken Souvlaki Salad Bowls (p. 53)
- Have your Basic Meatballs (p. 101) with Marinara Sauce (p. 117) on a bed of Zoodles (p. 82) instead of Roasted Spaghetti Squash (p. 83)
- Make Taco Salad Bowls (p. 56) with Braised Beef (p. 105) instead of Taco Meat (p. 107)
- Add Grilled Chicken Breast (p. 98) to Your Fish Scampi with Garlic Butter Zoodles (p. 30) instead of fish

But more than that, you can use this cookbook as a tool for near-unlimited meal inspiration. What I mean is, take your favorite way to prepare meat (protein), pair it with a side dish you love (carbohydrates), and add a yummy sauce (fat). With a variety of meat, side dish, and sauce options, you have a huge variety to choose from!

A few ideas:

- Pair Grilled Chicken Breast (p. 98), Creamy Mushroom Sauce (p. 114), and Zoodles (p. 82) for a creamy-pasta-type dish
- Combine Grilled Steak (p. 99), Teriyaki Sauce (p. 115), and Cauliflower Rice (p. 85) for a delicious keto take on Japanese takeout
- Serve Grilled Chicken (p. 98) with BBQ Sauce (p. 116) and Creamy Slaw (p. 89) for a delicious summer BBQ meal
- Instead of cheeseburgers in your Cheeseburger Salad Bowls (p. 45), use Grilled Chicken Breast (p. 98) and Baked Beef Bacon (p. 100)

CHAPTER 4

How to Meal Prep Power Bowls

Not only do keto power bowls provide a ton of fresh, new, and exciting low-carb high-fat meal inspirations, they also help save time and money by being meal-prep-friendly.

Tips to Meal Prep Breakfast Bowls

- Choose meals that have hard-boiled eggs or omelet bites instead of eggs cooked other ways as they keep better. You can also fry eggs ahead of time, but the yolk will harden as it cools and is reheated. Scrambled eggs are best when eaten right away after making, otherwise they can get rubbery if reheated.
- For breakfast bowls with a protein (like sausage or grilled steak) and a salad, store the components in separate glass containers.

To Meal Prep Salad Bowls

- Make a big batch of Leafy Greens Mix (p. 87) and keep it in the fridge for use all week. The best way to store greens in the fridge is to line a large glass container with paper towels, add the greens, and cover the container.
- Keep different components of a salad separate until you're ready to eat it. (Bento bowls work great here!)

To Meal Prep Soup and Stew Bowls

1. Divide the soup or stew into individual portions in glass containers, and stash them in the fridge or freezer (label them if they're going into the freezer).
2. If they were frozen, thaw them in the fridge overnight before eating.
3. Reheat on the stovetop or in the microwave.
4. Add any garnishes right before serving.

To Meal Prep Sides and Bases; Proteins; and Sauces, Dressings, and Condiments

One of the easiest ways to use this book as a meal prep tool is to make a couple of different proteins on your meal prep day (for example, Braised Beef (p. 105) and Grilled Chicken Breast (p. 98)), along with a few different sides (maybe Fajita Vegetables

(p. 91) and Cauliflower Rice (p. 85)). This way, you can easily whip up things like Chicken Fajita Salad Bowls (p. 51) and Cilantro Lime Shredded Beef Cauliflower Rice Bowls with Garlicky Guacamole (p. 34) in a matter of minutes.

Grilled Steak (p. 99) is another great choice to meal prep; it's delicious for breakfast (for example, Grilled Steak with Roasted Broccoli and Hollandaise [p. 20]), dinner (such as Grilled Steak with Cauliflower Rice and Creamy Mushroom Sauce [p. 35]), and everything in between.

Sauces, Dressings, and Condiments are also good to make ahead so they're ready for you whenever you're about to eat. Make up a few varieties and keep them in the fridge (if you'll be eating them that week) or in the freezer (if it's a freezer-friendly item). Here's a pro tip: freeze things like marinara sauce and teriyaki sauce portioned out in an ice cube tray, so you just have to grab a cube and you're all set!

CHAPTER 5

How to Use Power Bowls to Achieve Your Health Goals (Weight Maintenance, Weight Loss, and Weight Gain)

The first thing you should do is calculate your macronutrient requirements based on your specific health goals. Like any other diet or meal plan, whether you lose, gain, or maintain your weight is based on calories in versus calories out. To lose weight, you need to eat fewer calories than you burn. To gain weight, you need to eat more calories than you burn.

Once you know how many calories you need, you can see how many grams of fat, protein, and carbohydrates you should consume using a macronutrient calculator to keep your body in a state of nutritional ketosis. After that, it's easy to plug the power bowl recipes from this book into your eating plan.

Of course, it's very important to consult with a doctor before starting a new meal plan or way of eating. Additionally, you should have your doctor continue to monitor you as you progress with your diet. Also, note that weight loss, weight gain, and weight maintenance is a science, and you should consult a specialist for assistance with this. This cookbook is just a general tool to help you reach your goals.

Lastly, it can be very helpful to use a ketogenic tracking app, such as Cronometer, to help you make sure you're eating the right foods in the right quantities.

Using Power Bowls to Lose Weight

To lose weight, you will need to eat fewer calories than you burn. In other words, you'll need to be at a caloric deficit. Experts recommend reducing calories by about 500 to 1,000 per day, resulting in a more sustainable, slower-paced weight loss of about 1 to 2 pounds per week. There are two main ways you can achieve a calorie deficit: 1) exercising and/or 2) eating fewer calories. (Note that both should be monitored by a doctor!)

When it comes to eating keto power bowls, reducing your calories by 500 to 1,000 per day can be as easy as slightly reducing your portion size. The nice thing about reducing your portions but not eliminating a certain ingredient is that the macronutrient ratios remain the same.

Another possible way to reduce your daily calorie intake is to keep portion size the same, but scale back on fats, such as oil, butter, cheese, etc. The thing to note about cutting down on fats is that you want to make sure you're keeping your macronutrient intake within your personal macro requirements to keep your body in ketosis.

Using Power Bowls to Gain Weight

To gain weight, in general, you should eat more calories than you burn. Of course, if you're trying to build muscle, exercise and weight-lifting comes into play, but that's a different topic for a different book! We're just going to focus on using this cookbook as a tool to gain weight; namely, by eating more.

If you're trying to build lean muscle mass and gain weight, you will likely want to increase your proportion of meat, and also slightly increase your calories. In terms of how that relates to the recipes in this book, simply add more meat and keep the rest of the recipe the same. Note that how much more meat to add depends on your body's specific needs.

Using Power Bowls to Maintain Your Weight

In theory, it should be fairly easy to use the recipes in this cookbook to maintain your current weight. If you know your Basal Metabolic Rate (BMR), you know how many calories your body needs to keep functioning at rest. If you also determined your body's macronutrient requirements, you know what percentage of your calories should come from fat, protein, and carbohydrates. Just plug the recipes from this cookbook as-is into your daily eating wherever they fit in!

* * *

Ultimately, *Keto Power Bowls* will help you put together nutrient-dense, low-carb high-fat meals that fit into one beautiful bowl! With a variety of options at your fingertips, I hope you'll find this cookbook to be a great tool that will help you never get bored with your meal plan. And we all know that when we're not bored with our eating plan, we'll stay on track. And that's really the point of any diet or way of eating, right?

Happy keto-power-bowl-ing, friends! I hope you love these easy, nutritious, and delicious meals as much as I do.

xoxo, Faith

Breakfast Bowls

Fried Eggs and Baked Beef Bacon with Cauliflower Rice Hash

YIELDS 4 SERVINGS | PREP TIME: 5 MINUTES | COOK TIME: 10 MINUTES

Cauliflower Rice Hash

1 batch Cauliflower Rice (p. 85)

1 teaspoon onion powder

1 teaspoon garlic powder

¼ teaspoon sweet paprika

Fried Eggs

1 tablespoon avocado oil

4 large eggs

Others

1 batch Baked Beef Bacon (p. 100)

4 teaspoons minced fresh parsley

1. For the cauliflower rice hash, make the Cauliflower Rice as directed. When you add the salt and pepper, stir in the onion powder, garlic powder, and sweet paprika. Continue cooking until the cauliflower starts to brown in spots, about 2 minutes.

2. For the fried eggs, heat the oil in a medium nonstick skillet over high heat. Once hot, carefully crack the eggs into the skillet. Cook until the eggs are set according to your preference (don't flip them for sunny-side-up!).

3. To serve, divide the cauliflower rice hash among 4 shallow bowls. Top each with one-quarter of the Baked Beef Bacon, 1 fried egg, and 1 teaspoon minced fresh parsley.

Poached Eggs with Turkey Breakfast Sausage Patties and Summer Squash Breakfast Hash

YIELDS 4 SERVINGS | PREP TIME: 5 MINUTES | COOK TIME: 10 MINUTES

Summer Squash Breakfast Hash

2 tablespoons extra-virgin olive oil

2 medium yellow summer squash, cubed

½ teaspoon salt

½ teaspoon garlic powder

½ teaspoon onion powder

¼ teaspoon smoked sweet paprika

¼ teaspoon black pepper

Others

8 Turkey Breakfast Sausage Patties (p. 106)

4 eggs, poached

4 teaspoons minced fresh parsley

1. For the summer squash breakfast hash, heat the oil in a large, deep skillet over medium-high heat. Once hot, add the squash, salt, garlic powder, onion powder, smoked sweet paprika, and black pepper, and cook until the squash is fork-tender and starting to turn golden in spots, about 7 to 10 minutes, stirring occasionally. Divide the summer squash breakfast hash among 4 shallow bowls.

2. To serve, top each with 2 Turkey Breakfast Sausage Patties, 1 poached egg, and 1 teaspoon minced fresh parsley. Serve immediately.

Creamy Porridge with Berries and Coconut

Porridge

1 cup water

4 tablespoons unsweetened coconut flakes

3 tablespoons almond flour

2 tablespoons golden flaxseed meal

¼ teaspoon psyllium husk powder

1 pinch salt

10 drops liquid stevia

1 teaspoon vanilla extract

Toppings

2 tablespoons unsweetened coconut flakes

2 tablespoons frozen red raspberries

1. Add all ingredients for the porridge to a small saucepan over medium heat, and cook until it's bubbling vigorously around the edges.

2. Once it starts bubbling around the outside, continue cooking for 1 minute, stirring constantly.

3. Divide the porridge into 2 individual bowls and top each with 1 tablespoon unsweetened coconut flakes and 1 tablespoon frozen red raspberries. Serve warm.

Grilled Steak with Roasted Broccoli and Hollandaise

YIELDS 4 SERVINGS | PREP TIME: 5 MINUTES | COOK TIME: N/A

1 batch Grilled Steak (p. 99), thinly sliced across the grain

1 batch Roasted Broccoli (p. 86)

½ batch Easy Hollandaise (p. 121)

2 teaspoons minced fresh herbs, such as parsley or dill

1. Divide the Grilled Steak among 4 shallow bowls. Top with the Roasted Broccoli, Easy Hollandaise, and fresh herbs. Serve immediately.

Creamy Shakshuka Baked Eggs

YIELDS 1 SERVING | PREP TIME: 5 MINUTES | COOK TIME: 20 MINUTES

Butter, for the gratin dish

3 tablespoons homemade Marinara Sauce (p. 117)

¼ teaspoon crushed red pepper flakes

¼ teaspoon cumin

¼ teaspoon coriander

⅛ teaspoon sweet paprika

3 tablespoons heavy cream

2 large eggs

2 tablespoons crumbled feta

2 tablespoons fresh minced parsley, divided

1 pinch black pepper

1. Preheat the oven to 400°F. Butter a 12-ounce gratin dish.

2. Stir together the homemade Marinara Sauce, crushed red pepper flakes, cumin, coriander, and sweet paprika in a small bowl. Spread this out in the bottom of the prepared gratin dish.

3. Pour the cream on top of the marinara, and carefully crack in the eggs. Sprinkle on the feta, half the parsley, and the black pepper.

4. Bake until the egg whites are set and the yolk is cooked to your desired level, about 10 to 15 minutes.

5. Sprinkle on the remaining half of the parsley, and serve warm.

Huevos Rancheros
Fried Eggs with Fresh Salsa

YIELDS 1 SERVING | PREP TIME: 5 MINUTES | COOK TIME: 5 MINUTES

½ tablespoon avocado oil

2 large eggs

3 tablespoons Fresh Salsa (p. 123)

¼ avocado, sliced

2 tablespoons queso fresco

1 tablespoon thinly sliced scallion

1 tablespoon fresh cilantro leaves

1. Heat the oil in a small nonstick skillet over high heat. Once hot, carefully crack the eggs into the skillet. Cook until the eggs are set according to your preference (don't flip them for sunny-side-up!).

2. Transfer the eggs to a shallow bowl. Top with the Fresh Salsa, avocado, queso fresco, scallion, and cilantro leaves.

Herbed Baked Eggs

YIELDS 1 SERVING | PREP TIME: 5 MINUTES | COOK TIME: 20 MINUTES

½ tablespoon unsalted butter, plus more for the gratin dish

¼ small onion

1 small clove garlic, minced

¼ cup heavy cream

2 large eggs

2 tablespoons crumbled feta

2 tablespoons fresh minced herbs, such as parsley, dill, scallion, etc., divided

1 pinch black pepper

1 pinch crushed red pepper flakes

1. Preheat the oven to 400°F. Butter a 12-ounce gratin dish.

2. Heat ½ tablespoon of butter in a small skillet over medium heat. Once melted, add the onion and cook until starting to soften, about 3 minutes, stirring frequently. Add the garlic and cook 30 seconds more, stirring constantly. Spread this mixture into the bottom of the prepared gratin dish.

3. Pour the cream on top of the sautéed onion-garlic mixture, and carefully crack in the eggs. Sprinkle on the feta, half of the herbs, black pepper, and crushed red pepper flakes.

4. Bake until the egg whites are set and the yolk is cooked to your desired level, about 10 to 15 minutes.

5. Sprinkle on the remaining half of the fresh herbs, and serve warm.

Cheesy Omelet Bites with Leafy Greens and Bacon Vinaigrette

YIELDS 8 OMELET BITES (4 SERVINGS) | PREP TIME: 15 MINUTES | COOK TIME: 20 MINUTES

Cheesy Omelet Bites

5 large eggs

2 tablespoons minced fresh parsley

1 tablespoon minced fresh chives

⅛ teaspoon salt

⅛ teaspoon black pepper

3 ounces cheddar cheese, shredded (about ¾ cup)

Others

1 batch Leafy Greens Mix (p. 87)

1 batch Bacon Vinaigrette (p. 110)

1. Preheat the oven to 400°F. Line 10 muffin wells in a muffin tray with silicone liners.

2. To make the cheesy omelet bites, beat together the eggs, and then lightly beat in the parsley, fresh chives, salt, black pepper, and shredded cheddar.

3. Divide the egg mixture among the lined muffin wells. Bake until the eggs are puffed and golden, about 15 to 20 minutes.

4. To serve, toss together the Leafy Greens Mix and Bacon Vinaigrette. Serve the omelet bites on top of the dressed greens.

Dinner Bowls

Fish Scampi with Garlic Butter Zoodles

YIELDS 4 SERVINGS | PREP TIME: 15 MINUTES | COOK TIME: 3 MINUTES

2 tablespoons unsalted butter

2 cloves garlic, minced

1 batch Zoodles (p. 82)

½ teaspoon salt

⅛ teaspoon black pepper

1 batch Baked White Fish
(p. 103)

2 tablespoons pine nuts, toasted
in a dry skillet

2 tablespoons fresh-grated
Parmesan cheese

¼ cup fresh basil, leaves torn
right before serving

1. Heat the butter over medium-low; once hot, add the garlic and cook until fragrant, about 2 minutes, stirring constantly. Remove from heat.

2. Toss together the garlic butter, Zoodles, salt, and pepper in a large bowl.

3. Divide the Zoodles among 4 shallow bowls. Top each with a piece of fish and the pine nuts, Parmesan, and basil. Serve immediately.

Dilled Sausage and Sautéed Cabbage

YIELDS 4 SERVINGS | PREP TIME: 8 MINUTES | COOK TIME: 8 MINUTES

½ tablespoon avocado oil

4 fully-cooked turkey kielbasa sausage links (3 to 4 ounces)

1 batch Sautéed Cabbage (p. 96), warmed

4 tablespoons sour cream

4 tablespoons minced fresh dill

1. Preheat the oil in a large skillet over medium-high heat. Add the sausage and cook until browned, flipping to ensure even browning.

2. To serve, divide the cabbage among 4 shallow bowls. Top each with a sausage link, 1 tablespoon sour cream, and 1 tablespoon minced fresh dill.

Unstuffed Peppers Stir Fry Bowls

YIELDS 4 SERVINGS | PREP TIME: 15 MINUTES | COOK TIME: 15 MINUTES

2 tablespoons avocado oil

1 pound 90% lean ground beef

1 yellow onion, thinly sliced

1 green bell pepper, thinly sliced

5 cloves garlic, crushed or minced

1 tablespoon tomato paste

1 teaspoon dried Italian herb seasoning

1 teaspoon salt

¼ teaspoon black pepper

1⅓ cups prepared Cauliflower Rice (p. 85)

Fresh oregano leaves, for garnish (optional)

1. Heat the oil in a large skillet over high heat. Add the beef and cook until browned, about 6 to 8 minutes, stirring occasionally to break up the meat.

2. Add the onion and bell pepper, and cook until the vegetables start to soften, about 5 minutes, stirring occasionally.

3. Add the garlic, tomato paste, Italian herb seasoning, salt, and black pepper, and cook 1 minute more, stirring constantly.

4. To serve, add ⅓ cup of Cauliflower Rice to each individual bowl and top each with one-quarter of the stir fry. Garnish with fresh oregano leaves if desired.

Cilantro Lime Shredded Beef Cauliflower Rice Bowls with Garlicky Guacamole

YIELDS 4 SERVINGS | PREP TIME: 10 MINUTES | COOK TIME: N/A

Cilantro Lime Shredded Beef

½ batch Braised Beef (p. 105), warm

2 tablespoons fresh chopped cilantro

1 tablespoon fresh lime juice

1 teaspoon fresh lime zest

1 teaspoon ground coriander

1 teaspoon ground cumin

Others

1 batch Cauliflower Rice (p. 85), warm

2 batches Garlicky Guacamole (p. 120)

2 ounces crumbled queso fresco

1. To make the cilantro lime shredded beef, stir together the Braised Beef, cilantro, lime juice, lime zest, coriander, and cumin.

2. To serve, divide the Cauliflower Rice among 4 shallow bowls. Top each with one-quarter of the beef, Garlicky Guacamole, and queso fresco.

Grilled Steak with Cauliflower Rice and Creamy Mushroom Sauce

YIELDS 4 SERVINGS | PREP TIME: 5 MINUTES | COOK TIME: N/A

1 batch Cauliflower Rice (p. 85)

⅛ teaspoon sweet smoked paprika

1 batch Grilled Steak (p. 99), thinly sliced across the grain

½ batch Creamy Mushroom Sauce (p. 114)

4 teaspoons minced fresh parsley

1. Toss together the Cauliflower Rice and sweet smoked paprika in a bowl.

2. To serve, divide the Cauliflower Rice among 4 shallow bowls. Top each with one-quarter of the Grilled Steak, one-quarter of the Creamy Mushroom Sauce, and 1 teaspoon minced fresh parsley.

Basic Meatballs with Marinara Sauce and Spaghetti Squash

YIELDS 4 SERVINGS | PREP TIME: 10 MINUTES | COOK TIME: N/A

½ batch Roasted Spaghetti Squash (about 2½ cups total) (p. 83)

1 cup Marinara Sauce (p. 117)

1 batch Basic Meatballs (p. 101)

4 tablespoons freshly-grated Parmesan cheese

4 tablespoons fresh basil

1. Divide the spaghetti squash among 4 shallow bowls. Top each with ¼ cup Marinara Sauce, 4 meatballs, 1 tablespoon Parmesan cheese, and 1 tablespoon fresh basil.

Rosemary Lamb Greek Meatballs with Creamy Cucumber Salad

YIELDS 4 SERVINGS | PREP TIME: 10 MINUTES | COOK TIME: N/A

½ batch Leafy Greens Mix
(p. 87)

1 batch Basic Meatballs (p. 101)
(see note for variation)

1 batch Creamy Cucumber
Salad (p. 90)

1. Divide the Leafy Greens Mix among
4 shallow bowls. Top each with 4 meatballs
and one-quarter of the Creamy Cucumber
Salad.

NOTE

- For the meatballs, make this variation: use
ground lamb instead of ground beef. For
the herbs, use 1 tablespoon minced fresh
rosemary and 1 tablespoon minced fresh
oregano. Add ½ teaspoon fresh lemon zest.
Keep everything else in the Basic Meatballs
recipe the same.

Chili Garlic Steak Rice Bowl with Fried Egg

YIELDS 2 SERVINGS | PREP TIME: 10 MINUTES | COOK TIME: 10 MINUTES

Sesame Seed Cauliflower Rice

1½ cups Cauliflower Rice
(p. 85), warmed

½ tablespoon coconut aminos

½ teaspoon sesame seeds

Chili Garlic Steak

1 tablespoon avocado oil

1 cup cooked, chopped steak

2 large cloves garlic, minced or
crushed

¼ teaspoon crushed red pepper
flakes

¼ teaspoon salt

Others

1 tablespoon light sesame oil

2 fried eggs

2 scallions, green and white
parts, thinly sliced

1. For the sesame seed cauliflower rice, stir together the Cauliflower Rice, coconut aminos, and sesame seeds.

2. For the chili garlic steak, heat the oil in a medium skillet over medium heat. Add the steak, garlic, crushed red pepper flakes, and salt. Cook until the steak is warm and the garlic is fragrant, about 5 minutes, stirring frequently.

3. To serve, transfer the cauliflower rice to 2 individual bowls. Pour the chili garlic steak on top of each. Top each bowl with half of the light sesame oil, 1 fried egg, and half of the scallion.

Sweet and Sour Chicken Stir Fry Bowls

YIELDS 4 SERVINGS | PREP TIME: 14 MINUTES | COOK TIME: 16 MINUTES

Sweet and Sour Chicken

2 tablespoons avocado oil

1 pound boneless, skinless chicken breasts, thinly sliced

4 cloves garlic, crushed

1-inch piece fresh ginger, peeled and grated on a microplane

2 tablespoons coconut aminos

2 tablespoons Swerve Brown Sugar Replacement

1 tablespoon rice vinegar

¼ teaspoon crushed red pepper flakes

¼ teaspoon salt

⅛ teaspoon black pepper

Others

1 yellow onion, thinly sliced

1 red bell pepper, thinly sliced

½ pound sugar snap peas

1⅓ cups Cauliflower Rice (p. 85)

2 scallions, green and white parts, thinly sliced (optional)

1. Stir together all ingredients for the sweet and sour chicken in a large bowl. Cover and refrigerate 2 hours, or overnight.

2. Heat a large skillet over high heat. Add the sweet and sour chicken (and its marinating liquid) and cook until browned, about 8 to 10 minutes. Don't stir until the chicken is browned on the first side.

3. Add the onion and bell pepper, and cook until the vegetables start to soften, about 5 minutes, stirring occasionally.

4. Add the sugar snap peas and cook 1 minute more, stirring constantly.

5. To serve, add ⅓ cup of Cauliflower Rice to each bowl and top with one-quarter of the stir fry. Garnish with scallion if desired.

Chipotle Lime Fish Cauliflower Rice Bowls with Tangy Slaw

YIELDS 4 SERVINGS | PREP TIME: 10 MINUTES | COOK TIME: N/A

1 batch Baked White Fish (p. 103)

1 teaspoon fresh lime zest

1 teaspoon fresh lime juice

¼ teaspoon chipotle chile powder

1 batch Cauliflower Rice (p. 85)

½ batch Tangy Slaw (p. 89)

4 tablespoons crumbled queso fresco

4 tablespoons fresh cilantro leaves

1 lime, quartered

1. As soon as the fish is done baking, sprinkle on the lime zest, lime juice, and chipotle chile powder.

2. To assemble the bowls, divide the Cauliflower Rice among 4 shallow bowls. Top each with 1 piece of fish and one-quarter of the Tangy Slaw, crumbled queso fresco, and cilantro leaves. Garnish each with 1 lime wedge for squeezing on top.

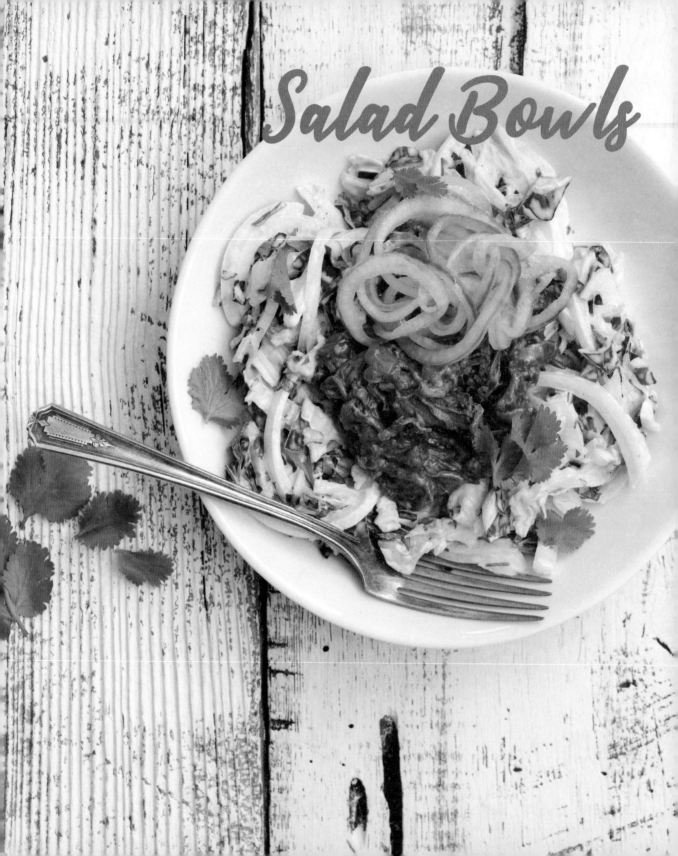

Salad Bowls

Cheeseburger Salad Bowls

YIELDS 4 SALADS | PREP TIME: 20 MINUTES | COOK TIME: N/A

Salad

8 cups chopped green leaf
  lettuce

1 large tomato, chopped

1 small red onion, halved and
  thinly sliced

4 ounces cheddar, shredded

⅓ cup dill pickles

8 slices Baked Beef Bacon
  (p. 100)

4 cooked Basic Burgers (p. 101),
  sliced

Dressing

4 tablespoons mayo

4 tablespoons sugar-free ketchup

4 tablespoons water

2 tablespoons dill relish

1 tablespoon yellow mustard

½ teaspoon Worcestershire sauce

⅛ teaspoon black pepper

1. Divide all the salad ingredients among
   4 individual salad bowls.

2. Whisk together all the dressing ingredients.

3. Serve the salad along with the dressing to
   drizzle on top.

Deconstructed Deviled Egg Salad

YIELDS 4 SERVINGS | PREP TIME: 20 MINUTES | COOK TIME: N/A

½ batch Leafy Greens Mix (p. 87)

½ batch Bacon Vinaigrette (p. 110)

8 hard-boiled eggs, peeled and halved

1 cup thinly sliced radishes

1 cup thinly sliced cucumber

1 stalk celery, thinly sliced on a diagonal

¼ small red onion, thinly sliced

4 tablespoons roasted red peppers, minced

4 tablespoons chopped fresh dill

2 tablespoons crumbled feta cheese

2 teaspoons capers, rinsed and patted dry

1. Toss together the Leafy Greens Mix and Bacon Vinaigrette. Divide the dressed greens among 4 shallow bowls.

2. To serve, top each dish of greens with 2 eggs (4 egg halves each) and one-quarter of the radish slices, cucumber slices, celery, red onion, roasted red peppers, dill, feta, and capers.

Chicken Caprese Salad Bowls with Balsamic Vinaigrette

YIELDS 4 SERVINGS | PREP TIME: 15 MINUTES | COOK TIME: 10 MINUTES

Chicken

½ cup water

2 tablespoons fresh lemon juice

2 tablespoons extra-virgin olive oil

2 large cloves garlic, peeled and cracked

1 teaspoon lemon zest

1 tablespoon minced fresh rosemary

½ teaspoon salt

¼ teaspoon black pepper

1 pound boneless, skinless chicken breasts, pounded into cutlets

Other

1 batch Leafy Greens Mix (p. 87)

1 batch Balsamic Vinaigrette (p. 111)

1 heirloom tomato, sliced

½ pound fresh mozzarella cheese, sliced

2 tablespoons toasted pine nuts

¼ cup fresh basil

1. Combine all ingredients for the chicken in a large bowl, and stir to coat the chicken. Cover and refrigerate for 2 to 4 hours. Remove the chicken from the marinade, and grill until fully cooked, about 8 to 10 minutes, flipping once halfway through (there should be no pink in the center). Let the chicken rest for 5 to 10 minutes after grilling.

2. To assemble the salad, toss together the Leafy Greens Mix and Balsamic Vinaigrette. Divide the dressed greens among 4 shallow bowls. Top each with one-quarter of the chicken, tomato, mozzarella, pine nuts, and fresh basil.

Teriyaki Green Bean Salmon Salad Bowls

YIELDS 4 SERVINGS | **PREP TIME: 15 MINUTES** | **COOK TIME: 15 MINUTES**

4 cups green beans, stems trimmed and chopped

1 cup low-sodium chicken stock

½ batch Leafy Greens Mix (p. 87)

1 batch Teriyaki Sauce (p. 115), divided

1 batch The Best Way to Cook Salmon (p. 102)

1 scallion, green and white parts, thinly sliced

1¼ teaspoons sesame seeds

1. Add the green beans and chicken stock to a large, deep skillet over medium-high heat. Cover the skillet and cook for 7 minutes. Uncover the skillet and cook for 3 minutes more. Turn the heat up to high and cook until the liquid is evaporated off, about 3 to 5 minutes more, stirring constantly. Remove from the heat.

2. To assemble the bowls, toss together the Leafy Greens Mix with half of the Teriyaki Sauce. Divide the dressed greens among 4 shallow bowls and top each with one-quarter of the green beans and 1 salmon fillet. Drizzle the remaining Teriyaki Sauce on top, and sprinkle on the scallion and sesame seeds.

Middle Eastern Style White Fish with Tahini Cucumber Salad

YIELDS 4 SERVINGS | PREP TIME: 10 MINUTES | COOK TIME: N/A

1 batch Baked White Fish
(p. 103)

½ teaspoon ground cumin

½ teaspoon ground coriander

1 batch Tahini Cucumber Salad
(p. 90)

1 lemon, quartered

1. Right before cooking the Baked White Fish, sprinkle the cumin and coriander on top.

2. Divide the Tahini Cucumber Salad among 4 shallow bowls. Top each serving with a piece of Baked White Fish. Serve each with a fresh lemon quarter to squeeze on top.

Chicken Fajita Salad Bowls

YIELDS 4 SERVINGS | PREP TIME: 20 MINUTES | COOK TIME: 10 MINUTES

Chicken

2 tablespoons avocado oil

2 tablespoons fresh lime juice

1 clove garlic, peeled and smashed but left intact (not minced or crushed)

1 teaspoon dried oregano

1 teaspoon ground cumin

¾ teaspoon salt

¼ teaspoon ancho chile powder

¼ teaspoon chipotle chile powder

½ teaspoon crushed red pepper flakes (more or less to taste)

¼ teaspoon ground black pepper

1 pound chicken breast, thinly sliced across the grain

Other

8 cups baby spinach

1 batch Fajita Vegetables (p. 91)

1 avocado, quartered

4 ounces queso fresco, crumbled

2 fresh limes, quartered, for squeezing on top

1. Mix together all ingredients for the chicken in a large zip-top bag. Put the bag inside a bowl and refrigerate for 2 to 24 hours. To cook the chicken, remove and discard the garlic clove. Preheat a large nonstick skillet over medium-high heat. Once hot, add the chicken and fully cook (there should be no pink inside), about 6 to 8 minutes, stirring occasionally.

2. To assemble the salad, put 2 cups baby spinach in the bottom of each bowl. Top each with one-quarter of the chicken, Fajita Vegetables, avocado, and 1 ounce of queso fresco.

3. Serve the salads along with the fresh lime wedges to squeeze on top.

Banh Mi Noodle Bowls

YIELDS 4 SERVINGS | PREP TIME: 25 MINUTES | COOK TIME: N/A

Dressing

2½ tablespoons avocado oil

1½ tablespoons rice vinegar

1 tablespoon coconut aminos

½ tablespoon toasted sesame oil

½ tablespoon Swerve Brown Sugar Replacement

¼ teaspoon crushed red pepper flakes

¼ teaspoon fish sauce

1 clove garlic, crushed

½ tablespoon freshly grated ginger

Spiralized Cucumber Salad

1 English cucumber, spiralized

1 small carrot, spiralized

½ small red onion, thinly sliced

1½ cups thinly sliced Savoy cabbage

½ cup fresh chopped cilantro

2 sprigs fresh chopped mint leaves

Others

1 batch Grilled Chicken Breast (p. 98), thinly sliced across the grain (see note)

1 red chile pepper, thinly sliced (optional)

1 tablespoon sesame seeds

1. Whisk together all ingredients for the dressing in medium bowl and set aside so the flavors can blend while you assemble the salad.

2. For the spiralized cucumber salad, divide all ingredients among 4 shallow bowls, arranging them nicely. Top with the chicken breast, sliced red chile pepper (if desired), and sesame seeds.

3. Drizzle the dressing on top and serve.

NOTE

- For a more complementary flavor profile, you can make a variation of the marinade used in the Grilled Chicken Breast (p. 98):

2 tablespoons water

1 tablespoon avocado oil

1 tablespoon coconut aminos

1 clove garlic, crushed

½ tablespoon freshly-grated ginger

½ tablespoon rice vinegar

½ tablespoon Swerve Brown Sugar Replacement

⅛ teaspoon crushed red pepper flakes

1 pound boneless, skinless chicken breasts

Chicken Souvlaki Salad Bowls

YIELDS 4 SERVINGS | PREP TIME: 25 MINUTES | COOK TIME: 15 MINUTES

Chicken

1 pound boneless, skinless chicken breasts

2 tablespoons fresh lemon juice

2 tablespoons extra-virgin olive oil

2 cloves garlic, crushed

1 teaspoon dried oregano

¼ teaspoon salt

¼ teaspoon black pepper

Tzatziki

6 tablespoons sour cream

3 tablespoons heavy whipping cream

2 teaspoons fresh lemon juice

½ clove garlic, crushed

¼ teaspoon dried dill

⅛ teaspoon black pepper

2 ounces feta cheese, crumbled

Salad

8 cups baby kale

½ seedless cucumber, thinly sliced

½ small green bell pepper, thinly sliced

½ small red onion, thinly sliced

½ cup cherry tomatoes, halved

¼ cup Kalamata olives, pitted

4 pepperoncini

1. Mix together all ingredients for the chicken in a large bowl; cover, and let it marinade for 2 hours in the fridge. Let the chicken sit at room temperature for 15 minutes before grilling. Grill until fully cooked, about 15 minutes, flipping once (there should be no pink in the center). Once cooked, let the chicken rest for 10 minutes before slicing across the grain.

2. While the chicken is marinating, mix together all ingredients for the tzatziki; cover and refrigerate until serving.

3. To assemble the salad, divide the vegetables for the salad and chicken among 4 bowls. Serve along with the tzatziki to spoon on top.

Pulled BBQ Beef Slaw Bowls

YIELDS 4 SERVINGS | PREP TIME: 10 MINUTES | COOK TIME: N/A

½ batch Braised Beef (p. 105), shredded with 2 forks (about 2 cups shredded)

4 tablespoons BBQ Sauce (p. 116)

1 batch Creamy Slaw (p. 89)

4 tablespoons Pickled Red Onions (p. 119)

2 tablespoons fresh cilantro leaves

1. Stir together the Braised Beef and BBQ Sauce in a medium bowl.

2. To assemble the bowls, divide the slaw among 4 shallow bowls. Top each with one-quarter of the beef mixture, Pickled Red Onions, and cilantro.

Taco Salad Bowls

YIELDS: 4 SALAD BOWLS (4 SERVINGS) | PREP TIME: 10 MINUTES | COOK TIME: N/A

1 batch Leafy Greens Mix (p. 87)

1 batch Taco Meat (p. 107)

2 ounces cheddar cheese, shredded (about ½ cup)

1 avocado, quartered and sliced

1 scallion, green and white parts, thinly sliced

4 tablespoons fresh cilantro leaves, for garnish

1. Assemble the salads by dividing the Leafy Greens Mix among 4 shallow bowls.

2. Top each with one-quarter of the Taco Meat, shredded cheese, avocado, scallion, and fresh cilantro leaves.

NOTE

- Serving Suggestion: If you have enough space to fit extra carbs into your daily macros, this salad is delicious topped with a serving of Fresh Salsa (p. 123)! And if you need to bump up your fat content, additional sour cream is the way to go here.

Soup and Stew Bowls

Indian Butter Chicken Bowls

YIELDS 6 SERVINGS | PREP TIME: 15 MINUTES | COOK TIME: 35 MINUTES

Chicken

1 pound boneless, skinless chicken breasts, cut into 1-inch cubes

3 tablespoons full-fat unflavored yogurt

1 tablespoon fresh lemon juice

2 cloves garlic, crushed

2 teaspoons garam masala spice mix

¼ teaspoon salt

Avocado oil spray, for the pan

Sauce

4 tablespoons unsalted butter

1 medium onion, chopped

4 large cloves garlic, minced

1 tablespoon fresh-grated ginger

1 tablespoon garam masala spice mix

1 teaspoon salt

1 teaspoon hot sauce

5 tablespoons tomato paste

2 cups low-sodium chicken stock

½ cup heavy whipping cream

10 drops liquid stevia

1 tablespoon fresh lemon juice

Others

2 cups prepared Cauliflower Rice (p. 85)

Fresh cilantro leaves (optional)

Diced red onion (optional)

1. To make the chicken, stir together the chicken, yogurt, lemon juice, garlic, garam masala, and salt in a large bowl. Cover and refrigerate 2 hours, or overnight.

2. Preheat the oven to 375°F. Lightly spray the bottom of a 9 by 13-inch casserole dish with avocado oil.

3. Let any excess liquid drip off the chicken, and then arrange it in an even layer in the prepared casserole dish. Bake until the chicken is fully cooked (there should be no pink inside), about 15 minutes.

4. To make the sauce, heat the butter in a large, deep skillet over medium to medium-high heat. Once melted, add the onion and cook 5 minutes, stirring occasionally. Stir in the garlic and ginger and cook 1 minute more, stirring constantly.

5. Stir in the garam masala, salt, hot sauce, tomato paste, and chicken stock. Turn the heat up and bring it to a boil, and then turn the heat down to simmer and cook (uncovered) 10 minutes, stirring occasionally.

6. Cool slightly, and then carefully puree the sauce in a blender or use an immersion blender. Return the sauce back to the skillet over medium heat.

7. Add the chicken and cook until warm, about 3 minutes. Stir in the cream, stevia, and lemon juice. Turn off the heat.

8. To serve, add ⅓ cup of Cauliflower Rice to each bowl and top each with one-sixth of the chicken mixture (about ¾ cup). Garnish with fresh cilantro leaves and diced red onion if desired.

Thai Coconut Curried Cod Bowls

YIELDS 4 SERVINGS | PREP TIME: 15 MINUTES | COOK TIME: 15 MINUTES

1 tablespoon avocado oil

1 small yellow onion, thinly sliced

½ medium red bell pepper, thinly sliced

1 medium yellow summer squash, halved lengthwise and thinly sliced

2 large cloves garlic, crushed or minced

½ tablespoon freshly grated ginger

1 teaspoon tamari sauce

½ teaspoon fish sauce

½ teaspoon crushed red pepper flakes (more or less to taste)

¼ teaspoon sea salt

2½ cups low-sodium fish stock

1 can full-fat unsweetened coconut milk

1 pound cod filets

Salt and pepper to taste

Fresh cilantro (optional)

Fresh lime wedges (optional)

1. Add the oil to a 3-quart saucepan over medium-high heat. Once hot, add the onion, bell pepper, and yellow squash, and cook until starting to soften, about 3 minutes, stirring occasionally.

2. Add the garlic and ginger and cook 30 seconds, stirring constantly.

3. Stir in the tamari sauce, fish sauce, red pepper flakes, salt, fish stock, and coconut milk.

4. Bring to a gentle simmer and then add the whole cod filets. Cover the saucepan, turn the heat down to simmer, and cook until the fish is opaque and flakes easily with a fork, about 10 minutes.

5. Taste and season with salt and pepper as desired. Serve garnished with fresh cilantro and lime wedges, if desired.

New England Fish Chowder

YIELDS 5 SERVINGS | PREP TIME: 25 MINUTES | COOK TIME: 35 MINUTES

2 tablespoons unsalted butter

2 slices beef bacon, chopped

1 small yellow onion, chopped

1 medium turnip (about ½ pound), peeled and chopped

1 small carrot, sliced

2 large stalks celery

3 cloves garlic, minced

2 teaspoons minced fresh thyme

3 cups low-sodium fish stock

1 bay leaf

½ teaspoon salt

⅛ teaspoon ground black pepper

1 cup heavy whipping cream

1 pound fresh white fish fillets, bones and skin removed (cod, haddock, or tilapia)

2 tablespoons minced fresh parsley, for garnish

1. Heat the butter in a 3-quart pot over medium heat. Once melted, add the bacon and sauté until it starts to get crispy, about 3 to 5 minutes, stirring occasionally. Add the onion, turnip, carrot, and celery, and cook until starting to soften, about 5 minutes, stirring occasionally. Add the garlic and thyme, and cook 1 minute, stirring constantly.

2. Add the fish stock, bay leaf, salt, and black pepper. Let it come up to a boil, and then turn the heat down to low, cover the pot, and simmer until the veggies are fork-tender, about 5 to 10 minutes.

3. Add the cream and the whole fish fillets, making sure they are completely submerged in liquid (they will break into smaller pieces while cooking). Cover the pot and cook (simmering) until the fish is fully cooked, about 10 to 15 minutes; don't stir until it's done. (Make sure it doesn't boil so the cream doesn't curdle.) The fish is done when it is opaque and flakes easily with a fork.

4. Taste the chowder and season with additional salt and black pepper as desired.

5. Garnish with parsley and serve.

NOTE

- *To Reheat:* Cook gently over low heat until warm, and avoid stirring. Be sure not to boil, as this can cause cream to curdle and the fish to completely disintegrate.

Cream of Broccoli Cheddar Soup

YIELDS 4 SERVINGS | PREP TIME: 8 MINUTES | COOK TIME: 18 MINUTES

1 tablespoon avocado oil

½ small yellow onion, finely diced

2 medium cloves garlic, crushed or minced

3 cups low-sodium chicken stock

½ teaspoon Worcestershire sauce

¼ teaspoon hot sauce

¼ teaspoon salt

¼ teaspoon black pepper

8 ounces cream cheese, room temperature and cut into cubes

1½ cups steamed broccoli florets

2 ounces shredded cheddar, divided

1 scallion, green and white parts, for garnish

1. Heat the oil in a medium saucepan over medium heat. Once hot, add the onion and cook until softened, about 5 to 7 minutes, stirring occasionally. Add the garlic and cook 1 minute more, stirring constantly.

2. Stir in the chicken stock, Worcestershire sauce, hot sauce, salt, and black pepper. Turn the heat up and bring to a boil, and then turn the heat back down to a simmer.

3. Whisk in the cream cheese a little at a time until the broth is smooth.

4. Stir in the broccoli and cook until warm, about 2 minutes.

5. Turn off the heat and stir in half the cheese.

6. Serve the soup with the remaining cheese and the scallion sprinkled on top.

Beanless Chili Bowls

YIELDS 5 SERVINGS | PREP TIME: 15 MINUTES | COOK TIME: 90 MINUTES

1 tablespoon avocado oil

1 pound beef stew meat

5 cups low-sodium beef stock

1 small yellow onion, chopped

4 large stalks celery, chopped

6 cloves garlic, minced

3 tablespoons minced fresh oregano

2 teaspoons cumin

1 teaspoon ancho chile powder

1 teaspoon chipotle chile powder

1 teaspoon salt

¼ teaspoon black pepper

5 tablespoons sour cream

5 teaspoons minced fresh chives

1. Add the avocado oil to a thick-bottomed soup pot over high heat. Pat the beef stew meat dry. Once the oil is hot, add the meat in an even layer and sear, about 4 minutes per side, flipping once. Sear the meat in 2 batches if needed to prevent overcrowding.

2. Add the beef stock and bring up to a boil. Turn the heat down to simmer, cover the pot, and cook until the meat is tender, but not falling apart, about 45 minutes to 1 hour.

3. Add the onion, celery, garlic, oregano, cumin, ancho chile powder, chipotle chile powder, salt, and black pepper. Bring back up to a boil, and then turn the heat down to simmer. Cover the pot and cook until the celery is fork-tender, about 20 to 30 minutes.

4. To serve, top each serving with 1 tablespoon sour cream and 1 teaspoon minced fresh chives.

Chicken Pistou Soup

YIELDS 8 SERVINGS | PREP TIME: 30 MINUTES | COOK TIME: 30 MINUTES

Soup

2 tablespoon extra-virgin olive oil

1½ pounds chicken breasts, cubed

1 small onion, chopped

1 large stalk celery, chopped

1 medium zucchini, chopped

1 cup peeled and chopped celeriac

1 cup quartered button mushrooms

1 Roma tomato (aka plum tomato), diced

4 cloves garlic, minced

1 tablespoon minced fresh thyme

6 cups low-sodium chicken stock

½ teaspoon salt

¼ teaspoon black pepper

Pistou

2 cloves garlic

¼ teaspoon salt

1 pinch black pepper

2 cups loosely packed fresh basil leaves

6 tablespoons extra-virgin olive oil

Others

8 tablespoons freshly grated Parmesan cheese, for garnish

1. For the soup, add the oil to a 5-quart pot over medium-high heat. Add the chicken and sear on both sides, about 5 minutes. Add the onion, celery, zucchini, celeriac, mushrooms, tomato, garlic, thyme, chicken stock, salt, and black pepper. Cover the pot and bring up to a boil, and then turn the heat down and simmer until the vegetables are tender, about 25 minutes.

2. For the pistou, pulse the garlic in a food processor until finely chopped. Add the salt and black pepper, and pulse two more times. Add the basil, and, with the motor running, drizzle in the olive oil, stopping to scrape down the sides as necessary.

3. Top each serving with 1 tablespoon freshly grated Parmesan cheese and one-eighth of the Pistou (about 1 tablespoon).

Rosemary Beef Vegetable Soup with Sour Cream and Chives Biscuits

YIELDS 8 SERVINGS | PREP TIME: 30 MINUTES | COOK TIME: 90 MINUTES

1½ tablespoons avocado oil

1½ pounds beef stew meat

8 cups low-sodium beef stock

1 bay leaf

1 small yellow onion, chopped

2 medium turnips (about 1.15 pounds), peeled and chopped

2 large stalks celery

1 medium carrot, sliced

5 cloves garlic, minced

3 tablespoons minced fresh rosemary

1 teaspoon Worcestershire sauce

1 teaspoon salt

¼ teaspoon black pepper

1 tablespoon beef gelatin, dissolved in 3 tablespoons boiling water

1 batch Sour Cream and Chive Biscuits (p. 95)

1. Add the avocado oil to a thick-bottomed soup pot over high heat. Pat the beef stew meat dry. Once the oil is hot, add the meat in an even layer and sear, about 4 minutes per side, flipping once. Sear the meat in 2 batches if needed to prevent overcrowding.

2. Add the beef stock and bay leaf, and bring up to a boil. Turn the heat down to simmer, cover the pot, and cook until the meat is tender, but not falling apart, about 45 minutes to 1 hour.

3. Add the onion, turnips, celery, carrot, garlic, rosemary, Worcestershire sauce, salt, and black pepper. Bring back up to a boil, and then turn the heat down to simmer. Cover the pot and cook until the vegetables are fork-tender, about 20 to 30 minutes.

4. Stir in the dissolved beef gelatin, and then turn off the heat.

5. Serve the soup along with the Sour Cream and Chive Biscuits.

Dessert Bowls

Kiwi Blackberry Smoothie Bowls

YIELDS 1 SERVING | PREP TIME: 10 MINUTES | COOK TIME: N/A

Smoothie
1 cup baby spinach

½ cup frozen blackberries

¼ organic kiwi, skin-on

4 tablespoons canned full-fat unsweetened coconut milk

1 tablespoon chia seeds

½ teaspoon vanilla extract

7 drops liquid stevia

1 pinch salt

Garnishes (Optional)
3 frozen blackberries

1 slice fresh kiwi

1 teaspoon unsweetened coconut flakes

1. Add the spinach to a blender, and then add the rest of the smoothie ingredients.

2. Blend until smooth, tamping down as necessary.

3. Transfer to a bowl and top with optional garnishes if desired.

Coconut Custard

YIELDS 4 SERVINGS | **PREP TIME: 10 MINUTES** | **COOK TIME: 25 MINUTES**

1 cup heavy whipping cream

½ cup water

3 tablespoons Swerve Confectioners

10 drops liquid stevia

1 pinch salt

6 large egg yolks

¼ teaspoon psyllium husk powder

3 tablespoons boiling water

1 teaspoon pure vanilla extract

1 teaspoon coconut extract

5 tablespoons unsweetened shredded coconut, divided

1. Heat the cream, water, Swerve Confectioners, liquid stevia, and salt in a medium saucepan over medium heat until it's steaming and starting to bubble around the outside.

2. Whisk 1 cup of the steaming hot cream mixture to the egg yolks to temper, starting with just a couple drops at first and gradually whisking in the whole 1 cup.

3. Pour the tempered egg yolk mixture into the cream mixture. Turn the heat down to low and cook until it boils, stirring constantly. Immediately turn off the heat.

4. Add the psyllium husk powder and boiling water to a small bowl and stir to dissolve.

5. Whisk the psyllium-husk-water mixture, vanilla, and coconut extract into the custard. Strain the custard through a fine mesh sieve.

6. Stir in 3 tablespoons shredded coconut.

7. Pour the custard into 4 small glasses. Lay a piece of plastic wrap directly on top of each custard. Cool to room temperature, and then refrigerate 2 hours before serving.

8. Right before serving, top each with ½ tablespoon shredded coconut.

Cheesecake Ice Cream Hot Fudge Sundaes

YIELDS 6 SERVINGS | PREP TIME: 12 MINUTES | COOK TIME: N/A

Cheesecake Ice Cream

4 ounces cream cheese, at room temperature

¼ cup water

¼ cup Swerve Confectioners

1½ teaspoons vanilla extract

¼ teaspoon fresh lemon juice

10 drops liquid stevia

¾ cup heavy whipping cream

Others

12 tablespoons Hot Fudge Sauce (p. 113), for topping

1. To make the cheesecake ice cream, beat together the cream cheese, water, Swerve Confectioners, vanilla, fresh lemon juice, and liquid stevia until smooth in a large bowl.

2. Beat the heavy cream to stiff peaks in a medium bowl.

3. Beat one-quarter of the whipped cream into the cream cheese mixture until smooth. Use a rubber spatula to fold in the remaining whipped cream, in one-quarter portions at a time.

4. Gently pour the mixture into a 9-inch loaf pan, lay a piece of plastic wrap directly on top, and freeze until stiffened enough to scoop, at least 4 hours or up to 2 weeks.

5. Let it set at room temperate for 10 to 15 minutes before scooping because this does freeze quite solid.

6. To serve, scoop ⅓ cup of cheesecake ice cream into an individual serving bowl and top with 2 tablespoons Hot Fudge Sauce.

Chocolate Pudding

YIELDS 3 SERVINGS | PREP TIME: 8 MINUTES | COOK TIME: N/A

1 medium-large ripe Hass avocado

⅓ cup unsweetened natural cocoa powder

⅓ cup heavy whipping cream

4 tablespoons stevia or monkfruit-sweetened maple-flavored syrup (such as Lakanto)

1 teaspoon pure vanilla extract

¼ teaspoon instant espresso powder, dissolved in ½ teaspoon warm water

1 pinch salt

1. Add all ingredients to a blender or food processor and puree until smooth, stopping to scrape down the sides as necessary.

2. Spoon into 3 small serving bowls or glasses and serve, or cover with plastic wrap and store refrigerated for up to 3 days before serving.

Strawberry Shortcake

YIELDS 6 SERVINGS | PREP TIME: 10 MINUTES | COOK TIME: 15 MINUTES

Strawberries

2 cups frozen strawberries, unthawed

¼ cup granulated erythritol

7 drops liquid stevia

1 pinch salt

1 teaspoon fresh lemon juice

½ teaspoon pure vanilla extract

Others

1 batch Sweet Shortcake Biscuits (p. 77)

6 tablespoons heavy whipping cream, whipped to soft peaks

1. For the strawberries, combine the strawberries, erythritol, liquid stevia, and salt in a large saucepan. Cover the saucepan and cook (covered) on the stovetop over medium heat for 10 minutes. Use a fork or potato masher to mash the berries, and continue cooking (uncovered) until the sauce is thickened to your desired consistency, about 2 to 5 minutes more, stirring frequently. Remove from the heat and stir in the lemon juice and vanilla extract.

2. To serve, split open each shortcake biscuit, spoon in one-sixth of the strawberry sauce (about 2 tablespoons), and top each with 1 tablespoon whipped cream.

Coconut Chocolate Trifles

YIELDS 10 SERVINGS | PREP TIME: 15 MINUTES | COOK TIME: N/A

2 batches Chocolate Pudding (p. 74)

½ cup unsweetened coconut flakes

1 batch Coconut Custard (p. 71)

2 tablespoons 90% cacao chocolate shavings

1. Divide the Chocolate Pudding among 10 small glass dessert bowls. Divide the coconut flakes on top. Spread the Coconut Custard on top. Sprinkle on the chocolate shavings.

2. Serve, or wrap and store in the fridge for up to 2 days before serving.

Sweet Shortcake Biscuits

YIELDS 6 BISCUITS | PREP TIME: 10 MINUTES | COOK TIME: 20 MINUTES

1½ cups almond flour

3 tablespoons Swerve Confectioners

1 teaspoon baking powder

¼ teaspoon psyllium husk powder

¼ teaspoon salt

4 tablespoons chilled unsalted butter, diced

1 large egg

2 teaspoons vanilla extract

10 drops liquid stevia

1. Preheat the oven to 350°F; line a large baking tray with parchment paper or a Silpat liner.

2. Whisk together the almond flour, Swerve Confectioners, baking powder, psyllium husk powder, and salt in a large bowl.

3. Use a fork or pastry cutter to cut the butter into the dry ingredient mixture until it looks like coarse meal (there should be some pieces the size of peas).

4. Lightly beat together the egg, vanilla, and liquid stevia in a small bowl.

5. Use a fork to mix the egg mixture into the almond flour mixture, being careful not to over-mix.

6. Roll the mixture into 6 equal-sized balls and arrange them on the prepared baking tray.

7. Bake the biscuits until they're puffed and golden on the bottom, about 16 to 20 minutes.

Faux Apple Crisp

YIELDS 8 SERVINGS | PREP TIME: 30 MINUTES | COOK TIME: 50 MINUTES

Zucchini Filling

1½ pounds zucchini (about
   3 small-to-medium-sized
   zucchini; about 4 cups sliced)

⅓ cup fresh lemon juice

1 cup Swerve Brown Sugar
   Replacement

10 drops liquid stevia

1½ teaspoons vanilla extract

2 teaspoons cinnamon

½ teaspoon nutmeg

¼ teaspoon salt

Crumble Topping

1 cup almond flour

2 tablespoons golden flaxseed
   meal

2 tablespoons Swerve Brown
   Sugar Replacement

¼ teaspoon salt

¼ teaspoon cinnamon

½ teaspoon vanilla extract

4 tablespoons chilled unsalted
   butter, diced

1 large egg white

4 tablespoons walnuts, chopped

1. Preheat the oven to 350°F.

2. For the zucchini filling, peel the zucchini. Trim off the ends, cut each zucchini in half lengthwise, and use a spoon to scrape out the seeds inside. Slice each zucchini in half crosswise into ¼-inch half-moons.

3. Add all the remaining ingredients and the zucchini to a large saucepan over medium heat. Cover the saucepan and cook until the zucchini is tender, but not mushy, about 20 to 25 minutes. As soon as it reaches a vigorous boil (this takes about 9 to 10 minutes), uncover the saucepan, turn the heat down slightly, and continue cooking uncovered, stirring occasionally.

4. Pour the zucchini mixture (and any liquid) into a 7 by 11-inch casserole dish (or equivalent size).

5. For the crumble topping, whisk together the almond flour, golden flaxseed meal, brown sugar replacement, salt, and cinnamon in a large bowl. Whisk in the vanilla. Cut in the butter with a fork or pastry cutter until it looks like coarse meal (there should be some pieces the size of peas). Mix in the egg white with a fork until crumbly. Stir in the walnuts.

6. Sprinkle the crumble topping on the zucchini filling.

7. Bake until the filling is bubbling and the topping is golden, about 25 minutes.

8. Serve warm or at room temperature. Store covered in the fridge for up to 5 days. Reheat in the microwave or in a 350°F oven until warm.

Vanilla Bean Cheesecake Mousse

YIELDS 6 SERVINGS | PREP TIME: 10 MINUTES | COOK TIME: N/A

8 ounces cream cheese

3 tablespoons Swerve Confectioners

1 teaspoon vanilla extract

½ teaspoon vanilla bean paste

10 drops liquid stevia

1 cup heavy cream

3 teaspoons finely chopped super dark chocolate (90% cacao)

1. Place the cream cheese in a large bowl, and microwave on high for 30 seconds to soften it. Add the Swerve Confectioners, vanilla, vanilla bean paste, and liquid stevia, and beat with a handheld electric mixer until smooth.

2. Beat the heavy cream to stiff peaks in a separate medium bowl. Beat one-quarter of the whipped cream into the cream cheese mixture until smooth. Use a rubber spatula to fold in the remaining whipped cream one-quarter portions at a time.

3. Transfer the mousse to 6 small glasses or bowls.

4. Serve, or cover and keep refrigerated up to 3 days before serving.

5. Right before serving, sprinkle ½ teaspoon finely chopped chocolate on top of each bowl.

Sides and Bases

Zoodles

1 pound (about 2 medium) zucchini

1. Use a spiralizer to make zoodles from the zucchini. If you don't have a spiralizer, use a vegetable peeler to make thin zucchini ribbons. You can also use a mandoline to thinly slice the zucchini and then stack the zucchini slices and cut them into long, thin strips.

NOTE

- Similar to "al dente" noodles, I like my zoodles to have a slight bite to them (no one likes mushy noodles, right?). I find that zoodles don't need to be cooked; I just toss them with whatever sauce I'm serving them with! If you really want to cook them, I recommend about 30 seconds to 1 minute in a skillet over medium to medium-high heat. Any longer than that and you run the risk of the zoodles becoming mushy and watery.

Roasted Spaghetti Squash

YIELDS 8 SERVINGS | PREP TIME: 10 MINUTES | COOK TIME: 60 MINUTES

1 (2 pound) spaghetti squash
1 tablespoon extra-virgin
  olive oil
¼ teaspoon salt
¼ teaspoon black pepper

1. Preheat the oven to 400°F and line a large baking sheet with foil.

2. Cut both ends off the spaghetti squash. Stand the squash up, carefully cut it in half lengthwise, and then scoop out the seeds. Rub the oil on the inside of both halves, and season with salt and pepper.

3. Place the squash halves cut-side-down on the prepared baking sheet. Roast until the squash is fork-tender but not mushy, about 40 to 60 minutes.

4. Use a metal spatula to flip the squash halves over (so they're cut-side-up), and let them sit until they're cool enough to handle.

5. Use a fork to scrape the stands out, gently fluffing them so they stay as strands and look like noodles.

Cauliflower Rice

YIELDS 4 SERVINGS | PREP TIME: 7 MINUTES | COOK TIME: 3 MINUTES

1 small head cauliflower (about 1¼ to 1½ pounds)

2 tablespoons avocado oil

¼ teaspoon salt

⅛ teaspoon black pepper

1. Trim the leaves off of the cauliflower head. Rinse the cauliflower under cool running water and pat dry.

2. Use a box grater to shred the cauliflower (the same side you'd use to shred cheese).

3. Heat a large skillet over medium to medium-high heat. Add the oil, and once hot, add the cauliflower. Cook until it's just starting to soften, about 3 minutes, stirring occasionally. Stir in the salt and pepper. Serve warm.

Roasted Broccoli

YIELDS 4 SERVINGS | PREP TIME: 5 MINUTES | COOK TIME: 20 MINUTES

2½ cups broccoli florets

4 teaspoons extra-virgin olive oil

¼ teaspoon salt

⅛ teaspoon black pepper

1. Preheat the oven to 425°F.

2. Toss together all ingredients on a large baking tray, and spread out the broccoli in an even layer.

3. Roast until the broccoli is fork-tender and starting to turn brown and crispy in spots, about 18 to 22 minutes (don't stir or flip the broccoli).

NOTES

Flavor Variations

- Lemon: Roast as directed, and toss the warm broccoli with 1 teaspoon fresh lemon zest.

- Parmesan: Roast as directed, and toss the warm broccoli with 2 tablespoons grated Parmesan cheese.

- Garlic: Mix 1 clove crushed garlic with 1 tablespoon extra-virgin olive oil. Halfway through roasting, drizzle the garlic oil on the broccoli and continue roasting.

Leafy Greens Mix

YIELDS 4 SERVINGS | PREP TIME: 5 MINUTES | COOK TIME: N/A

4 cups chopped kale

2 cups baby spinach

2 cups arugula

1. Toss together all ingredients.

2. Use as a base for your favorite salad, or store in the fridge for up to 3 days.

NOTE

- To store in the fridge, line a large glass container with paper towels. Spread the Leafy Greens Mix out on the paper towels. Cover the container (if the container doesn't have a lid, use plastic wrap), and store in the fridge for up to 3 days.

Slaw, Two Ways

YIELDS 4 SERVINGS | PREP TIME: 20 MINUTES | COOK TIME: N/A

Slaw

4 cups thinly sliced Napa
cabbage

1 cup thinly sliced red cabbage

¼ small yellow onion, thinly
sliced

¼ cup chopped fresh parsley

Dressing for Creamy Slaw

½ cup mayo

2 teaspoons apple cider vinegar

2 drops liquid stevia

½ teaspoon salt

¼ teaspoon hot sauce

⅛ teaspoon black pepper

Dressing for Tangy Slaw

4 tablespoons extra-virgin
olive oil

5 teaspoons apple cider vinegar

2 drops liquid stevia

½ teaspoon salt

⅛ teaspoon black pepper

1. Toss together all ingredients for the slaw.

2. To dress the slaw, choose either the creamy or tangy dressing and whisk together all ingredients for that dressing. Then toss the dressing with the slaw mixture.

3. Serve, or store covered in the fridge for up to 2 days. (Note that the vegetables will soften the longer the slaw sits.)

NOTE

• Make a double batch of the slaw mixture (8 servings), and make 1 batch of each of the different dressings. Divide the slaw mixture into 2 separate bowls, and dress each with the different dressing!

Cucumber Salad, Two Ways

YIELDS 4 SERVINGS | PREP TIME: 20 MINUTES | COOK TIME: N/A

Creamy Cucumber Salad

6 tablespoons sour cream

3 tablespoons heavy whipping cream

2 teaspoons fresh lemon juice

½ clove garlic, crushed

¼ teaspoon dried dill

¼ teaspoon salt

⅛ teaspoon black pepper

1 cucumber, thinly sliced

2 ounces feta cheese, crumbled

1. Whisk together the sour cream, heavy whipping cream, fresh lemon juice, garlic, dried dill, salt, and black pepper. Stir in the cucumber. Sprinkle the feta on top.

Tahini Cucumber Salad

¼ cup tahini

2 teaspoons fresh lemon juice

¼ cup water

¾ cucumber, diced

2 tablespoons minced white onion

¼ cup cherry tomatoes, diced

¼ bunch fresh parsley leaves, minced

2 sprigs fresh mint leaves, minced

¼ teaspoon salt

3 tablespoons olive oil

1. Whisk together the tahini and lemon juice in a medium bowl.

2. Whisk the water into the tahini-lemon-juice mixture drop by drop at first, and then in a thin drizzle (the sauce will thicken and then thin out into a smooth, pourable consistency).

3. Stir the tahini dressing together with all the remaining ingredients (except the olive oil) in a medium bowl. Refrigerate for 30 minutes so the flavors can blend.

4. Right before serving, drizzle the olive oil on top.

Fajita Vegetables

YIELDS 4 SERVINGS | **PREP TIME: 10 MINUTES** | **COOK TIME: 5 MINUTES**

1½ tablespoons avocado oil

½ green bell pepper, thinly sliced

½ red bell pepper, thinly sliced

1 small yellow onion, halved and thinly sliced

2 cloves garlic, minced

½ teaspoon cumin

½ teaspoon dried oregano

¼ teaspoon salt

¼ teaspoon ancho chile powder

¼ teaspoon chipotle chile powder

⅛ teaspoon black pepper

1. Add the avocado oil to a large nonstick skillet over medium-high heat.

2. Once hot, add the bell peppers and onion and cook until starting to soften and brown in spots, about 3 minutes, stirring occasionally.

3. Add the garlic, cumin, oregano, salt, ancho chile powder, chipotle chile powder, and black pepper, and cook 1 minute more, stirring constantly.

Wilted Garlicky Greens

YIELDS ABOUT 1 1/2 CUPS (4 SERVINGS) | PREP TIME: 10 MINUTES | COOK TIME: 10 MINUTES

2 tablespoons extra-virgin olive oil

4 cups chopped kale

½ cup low-sodium chicken or vegetable stock

⅛ teaspoon salt

⅛ teaspoon black pepper

2 cloves garlic, crushed

4 cups baby spinach

½ teaspoon fresh lemon zest

¼ teaspoon crushed red pepper flakes

⅛ teaspoon dried dill

1. Add the oil to a large skillet over medium-high heat. Once hot, add the kale, chicken or vegetable stock, salt, and black pepper. Cover the skillet and cook until the kale is tender and the liquid is mostly evaporated, about 4 to 5 minutes, stirring occasionally.

2. Add the garlic and spinach and cook uncovered until the spinach is wilted, about 4 to 5 minutes more, stirring frequently.

3. Turn off the heat and stir in the lemon zest, crushed red pepper flakes, and dried dill.

Sour Cream and Chive Biscuits

1 cup almond flour

1 teaspoon baking powder

¼ teaspoon psyllium husk powder

¼ teaspoon salt

⅛ teaspoon black pepper

2 tablespoons chilled unsalted butter, diced

¼ cup shredded mozzarella cheese

3 tablespoons sour cream

2 tablespoons minced fresh chives

1. Preheat the oven to 350°F; line a large baking tray with parchment paper or a Silpat liner.

2. Whisk together the almond flour, baking powder, psyllium husk powder, salt, and black pepper in a large bowl.

3. Use a fork or pastry cutter to cut the butter into the dry ingredients until it looks like coarse meal (there should be some pieces the size of peas). Mix in the shredded mozzarella with a fork, and then mix in the sour cream with a fork. Stir in the chives.

4. Cover the dough and chill in the freezer for 10 minutes.

5. Divide the dough into 8 equal pieces. Roll each into a ball and arrange the balls on the prepared baking tray.

6. Bake the biscuits until they're puffed and golden on the bottom, about 15 to 17 minutes.

Sautéed Cabbage

YIELDS 4 SERVINGS | PREP TIME: 10 MINUTES | COOK TIME: 25 MINUTES

1 tablespoon unsalted butter

1 tablespoon avocado oil

8 cups thinly sliced green cabbage (1 small head cabbage, about 1½ to 1¾ pounds)

2 cloves garlic, minced

1 tablespoon apple cider vinegar

¾ cup low-sodium chicken stock or vegetable stock

½ teaspoon salt

⅛ teaspoon black pepper

1 tablespoon minced fresh parsley

1. Heat the butter and oil in a 5-quart pot over medium heat.

2. Add the cabbage, garlic, apple cider vinegar, chicken stock, salt, and black pepper, and cook until the cabbage is starting to wilt, about 5 minutes, stirring occasionally.

3. Cover the pot and cook until the cabbage is tender, about 20 minutes, stirring occasionally and adding a splash of water as necessary if the pot gets too dry.

4. Taste and add additional salt and pepper if desired. Sprinkle the parsley on top and serve.

Grilled Chicken Breast

YIELDS 4 SERVINGS | PREP TIME: 5 MINUTES | COOK TIME: 15 MINUTES

1 pound boneless, skinless chicken breasts

2 tablespoons fresh lemon juice

2 tablespoons extra-virgin olive oil

¼ teaspoon salt

¼ teaspoon black pepper

1. Mix together all ingredients in a large bowl; cover, and let it marinade for 2 hours in the fridge.

2. Let the chicken sit at room temperature for 15 minutes before grilling.

3. Grill over medium-high heat until fully cooked, about 15 minutes, flipping once (there should be no pink in the center and the internal temperature should be 165°F). You can cook the chicken on a grill pan inside or on an outdoor grill.

4. Once cooked, let the chicken rest for 5 to 10 minutes.

Grilled Steak

2 (1 pound) bone-in ribeye
  steaks
½ teaspoon salt
¼ teaspoon black pepper

1. Let the steak sit at room temperature for
   15 minutes before grilling. Season both sides
   of each steak with the salt and pepper.

2. Sear the steaks over high heat, about
   3 minutes per side. Turn the heat down to
   medium-low and continue cooking until they
   reach your desired level of doneness (about
   145°F for "medium").

3. Once cooked, let the steak rest for
   5 to 10 minutes.

Baked Beef Bacon

YIELDS 4 SERVINGS (ABOUT 2 SLICES PER SERVING) | **PREP TIME: 3 MINUTES** | **COOK TIME: 15 MINUTES**

1 tablespoon avocado oil

8 ounces uncured beef bacon (beef navel)

1. Preheat oven to 400°F; line a large baking tray with foil.

2. Drizzle the oil onto the baking tray. Arrange the bacon in an even layer.

3. Bake until the bacon is crispy, about 15 minutes (no need to flip it).

Basic Meatballs or Burgers

Avocado oil spray

1 pound 85% lean ground beef

1 tablespoon extra-virgin
olive oil

½ small yellow onion, grated

½ teaspoon salt

¼ teaspoon black pepper

3 tablespoons minced fresh
herbs, such as parsley,
rosemary, oregano, basil,
chives, etc.

1. Preheat the oven to 375°F; lightly spray a
large baking tray with avocado oil.

2. Use your hands to combine all remaining
ingredients in a large bowl.

3. For meatballs, roll the meat mixture into
16 meatballs and place them on the prepared
baking sheet. For burgers, shape the meat
mixture into 4 patties and place them on the
prepared baking sheet.

4. Bake until fully cooked, about
15 to 20 minutes.

The Best Way to Cook Salmon

YIELDS 4 SERVINGS | PREP TIME: 2 MINUTES | COOK TIME: 8 MINUTES

4 (6 ounce) skin-on salmon
  fillets
¼ teaspoon salt
⅛ teaspoon black pepper
2 teaspoons avocado oil

1. Preheat the oven to 425°F.

2. Preheat a large, nonstick, oven-safe skillet over medium-high heat.

3. Pat the salmon fillets dry on both sides, and season with salt and pepper.

4. Add the oil to the hot skillet, and add the salmon fillets, skin-side down. Tent the top of the skillet with foil.

5. Cook until the skin is browned, about 3 to 4 minutes. (Do not flip.)

6. Transfer the skillet (still tented with foil) to the preheated oven and cook for 4 to 5 minutes more. The salmon is done when it's opaque and flakes easily with a fork.

7. Remove the skillet from the oven and let it sit (still tented with foil) for 3 minutes. (The salmon will continue cooking during this step.)

Baked White Fish

YIELDS 4 SERVINGS | **PREP TIME: 5 MINUTES** | **COOK TIME: 17 MINUTES**

2 tablespoons extra-virgin olive oil, divided

4 (6 ounce) white fish fillets, such as cod or haddock

¼ teaspoon salt

⅛ teaspoon black pepper

1 lemon, cut into wedges

1. Preheat the oven to 375°F. Brush the bottom of a 9 by 13-inch glass dish with ½ of tablespoon extra-virgin olive oil.

2. Pat the white fish fillets dry with paper towels. Brush the remaining 1½ tablespoons of oil and the salt and pepper on both sides of each fish fillet.

3. Arrange the fish in the prepared baking dish and bake until it's opaque and flakes easily with a fork, about 15 to 17 minutes.

4. Serve each piece along with a lemon wedge to squeeze on top.

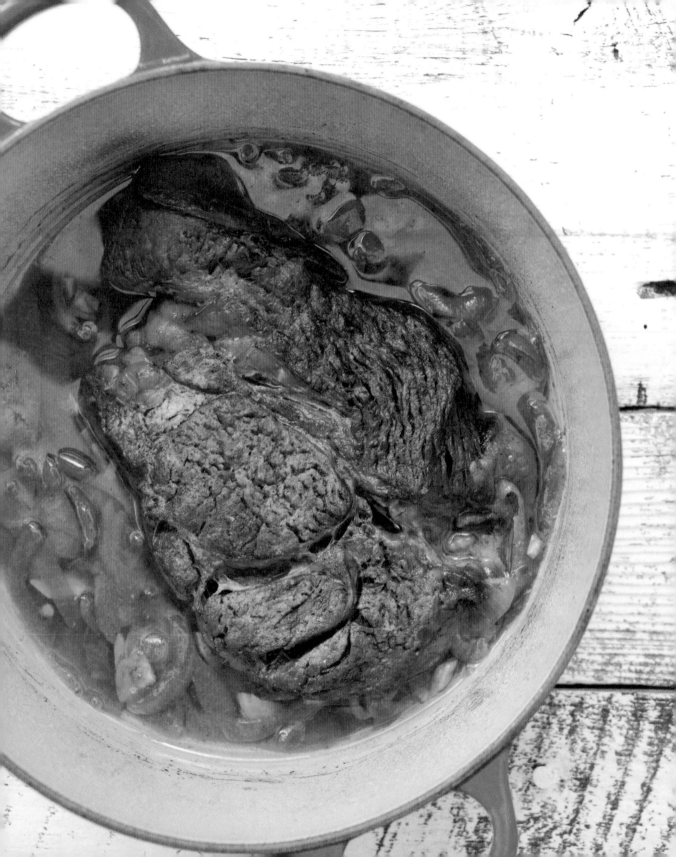

Braised Beef

1 (2-pound) beef chuck roast

½ teaspoon salt

½ teaspoon black pepper

2 tablespoons avocado oil

1 cup low-sodium beef stock

½ medium yellow onion, thinly sliced

2 cloves garlic, minced

1 bay leaf

1. Preheat the oven to 275°F.

2. Pat the beef chuck roast dry with paper towels, and season both sides with salt and pepper.

3. Heat the oil in a 5-quart Dutch oven over high heat. Once hot, sear the meat until browned, about 2 minutes per side, flipping once.

4. Add the beef stock, onion, garlic, and bay leaf.

5. Cover the Dutch oven, and cook until the meat is so tender it falls apart, about 4 to 5 hours.

6. To make shredded or pulled beef, simply shred the beef with 2 forks (you will get about 4 cups of shredded meat).

Turkey Breakfast Sausage Patties

**YIELDS 10 SAUSAGE PATTIES (5 SERVINGS) | PREP TIME: 12 MINUTES |
COOK TIME: 12 MINUTES**

1 pound ground turkey

½ small yellow onion, grated

1 tablespoon stevia or monkfruit-sweetened maple-flavored syrup (such as Lakanto)

1 teaspoon minced fresh thyme

¾ teaspoon salt

½ teaspoon fennel seeds

½ teaspoon apple cider vinegar

¼ teaspoon ground sage

¼ teaspoon black pepper

4 teaspoons extra-virgin olive oil, divided

1. Add all ingredients, except the olive oil, to a large bowl and use your hands to mix until combined, being careful not to overmix.

2. Divide the meat mixture into 10 equal balls, and then shape each into a patty about 3 inches in diameter.

3. Heat a large nonstick skillet over medium to medium-high heat. Once hot, add 2 teaspoons of extra-virgin olive oil. Add half of the patties and cook until browned on the first side, about 3 minutes. Flip, turn the heat down to medium-low, and continue cooking until browned on the second side and fully cooked inside, about 3 minutes more. Transfer the cooked patties to a plate.

4. Add the remaining 2 teaspoons of oil to the same skillet, and cook the remaining sausage patties the same way. Serve warm.

Taco Meat

1 pound 85% lean ground beef

½ small onion, diced

4 large cloves garlic, crushed

1½ teaspoons cumin

1 teaspoon salt

1 teaspoon dried oregano

½ teaspoon ancho chile powder

½ teaspoon chipotle chile powder

¼ teaspoon black pepper

2 tablespoons tomato paste

3 drops liquid stevia

1. Add the beef and onion to a medium-large skillet over medium-high heat. Cook until the meat is browned, about 6 to 8 minutes, stirring occasionally with a wooden spoon to break up the meat.

2. Add the garlic, cumin, salt, dried oregano, ancho chile powder, chipotle chile powder, black pepper, tomato paste, and liquid stevia. Cook 2 to 3 minutes more, stirring constantly.

Sauces, Dressings, and Condiments

Dijon Vinaigrette

YIELDS 4 SERVINGS | PREP TIME: 3 MINUTES | COOK TIME: N/A

4 tablespoons extra-virgin olive oil

1½ tablespoons apple cider vinegar

½ teaspoon Dijon mustard

1 drop liquid stevia

⅛ teaspoon salt

⅛ teaspoon black pepper

1. Whisk together all ingredients to combine.

2. Use the vinaigrette to dress salad.

NOTE

- To make Bacon Vinaigrette: omit the salt. Add 2 tablespoons minced crispy-cooked bacon.

Balsamic Vinaigrette

4 tablespoons extra-virgin olive oil

2 tablespoons balsamic

3 drops liquid stevia

⅛ teaspoon salt

⅛ teaspoon black pepper

1. Whisk together all ingredients to combine.

2. Use the vinaigrette to dress salad.

Hot Fudge Sauce

YIELDS ABOUT 1 CUP/8 (2-TABLESPOON) SERVINGS | PREP TIME: 7 MINUTES |
COOK TIME: 3 MINUTES

¾ cup heavy whipping cream

½ cup + 2 tablespoons
unsweetened cocoa powder,
sifted

⅓ cup Swerve Brown Sugar
Replacement

1 ounce stevia-sweetened dark
chocolate, chopped

1 tablespoon unsalted butter

¾ teaspoon vanilla extract

1 pinch salt

1 pinch espresso powder

1. Whisk together all ingredients in a small
saucepan.

2. Cook over medium heat until the butter
and chocolate are melted, and the sauce
is smooth, about 3 minutes, whisking
frequently.

3. Cool to room temperature and then store in a
lidded jar in the fridge for up to 2 weeks.

4. To reheat, spoon the amount desired
into a microwave-safe bowl and heat for
15 seconds. Stir, and then heat for an
additional 10 seconds if needed. Or reheat
in a small saucepan over medium-low heat,
stirring constantly.

NOTE

- Serving suggestion: serve on top of
Cheesecake Ice Cream (p. 73).

Creamy Mushroom Sauce

YIELDS 4 SERVINGS | PREP TIME: 5 MINUTES | COOK TIME: 10 MINUTES

2 tablespoons unsalted butter

8 ounces whole button mushrooms, quartered

3 cloves garlic, minced

½ cup water, plus more as needed to thin out the sauce

3 ounces cream cheese

½ teaspoon Worcestershire sauce

⅛ teaspoon black pepper

Salt to taste

1 teaspoon minced fresh parsley, for garnish

1. Heat the butter in a medium skillet over medium to medium-high heat. Once hot, add the mushrooms and cook until softened and starting to brown, about 5 minutes, stirring frequently.

2. Turn the heat down to low, add the garlic, and cook 1 minute, stirring constantly.

3. Add the water, and use a wooden spoon to scrape up any brown bits that have formed on the bottom of the skillet.

4. Stir in the cream cheese, Worcestershire sauce, and black pepper, and cook until heated throughout, about 3 minutes, stirring constantly. Add a splash more water if the sauce is too thick.

5. Taste and add salt if desired. Serve garnished with fresh parsley.

Teriyaki Sauce

1 tablespoon avocado oil

2 large cloves garlic, crushed

1-inch piece fresh ginger, grated

2 tablespoons coconut aminos

1 tablespoon stevia-sweetened maple-flavored syrup

½ tablespoon rice vinegar

½ teaspoon sesame seeds

¼ teaspoon toasted sesame oil

¼ teaspoon crushed red pepper flakes

1. Heat the oil in a small skillet over medium-low heat.

2. Once hot, add the garlic and ginger, and cook 1 minute, stirring constantly.

3. Add the coconut aminos, maple-flavored syrup, and vinegar. Bring to a simmer, and then cook 15 seconds, stirring constantly.

4. Remove from the heat and stir in the sesame seeds, sesame oil, and crushed red pepper flakes.

BBQ Sauce

YIELDS 1 1/2 CUPS, OR 12 (2-TABLESPOON) SERVINGS | PREP TIME: 10 MINUTES | COOK TIME: 15 MINUTES

6 ounces tomato paste

1 cup low-sodium chicken stock (or low-sodium vegetable stock)

3 tablespoons apple cider vinegar

2 tablespoons Swerve Brown Sugar Replacement

1½ tablespoons Worcestershire sauce

½ tablespoon Dijon mustard

½ tablespoon onion powder

½ tablespoon garlic powder

¼ teaspoon salt

¼ teaspoon black pepper

1 pinch cayenne pepper

10 drops liquid stevia

1. Stir together all ingredients in a deep saucepan over high heat.

2. Bring to a boil, and then cover but keep the lid ajar. Turn the heat down and simmer 10 to 15 minutes, stirring occasionally.

3. Remove from the heat. The sauce will thicken more as it cools.

4. Store covered in the fridge for up to 2 weeks.

Marinara Sauce

YIELDS 1 1/2 CUPS, 6 (1/4-CUP) SERVINGS | PREP TIME: 10 MINUTES |
COOK TIME: 25 MINUTES

4 tablespoons extra-virgin
  olive oil

6 large cloves garlic, crushed

1 cup finely chopped Roma
  tomatoes, with juices

1 cup water

¼ cup tomato paste

½ teaspoon dried basil leaves

¼ teaspoon salt

⅛ teaspoon black pepper

3 drops liquid stevia

10 fresh basil leaves

1. Heat the oil in a medium saucepan over medium-low heat. Once hot, add the garlic and cook until fragrant, about 2 to 3 minutes, stirring frequently.

2. Add the chopped Roma tomatoes, turn the heat up to medium, cover the saucepan, and cook 8 minutes, stirring occasionally.

3. Stir in the water, tomato paste, dried basil leaves, salt, black pepper, and liquid stevia. Bring to a boil over medium heat, and then turn the heat down slightly and cook (uncovered) until thickened, about 10 minutes, stirring occasionally.

4. Turn off the heat. Tear the fresh basil leaves with your hands and stir them into the sauce.

Pickled Red Onions

YIELDS 1 CUP PICKLED ONIONS | PREP TIME: 10 MINUTES | COOK TIME: N/A

1 cup thinly sliced red onion

1 cup water

5 tablespoons apple cider vinegar

½ teaspoon salt

¼ teaspoon whole peppercorns

12 drops liquid stevia

1. Add all ingredients to a glass mason jar, cover the jar, and refrigerate at least 4 hours.

2. Store in the fridge for up to 2 weeks.

Garlicky Guacamole

YIELDS 6 SERVINGS | PREP TIME: 7 MINUTES | COOK TIME: N/A

2 Haas avocados, halved and peeled

2 large cloves garlic, crushed

2 tablespoons fresh lemon juice

2 tablespoons chopped fresh cilantro, plus a few more leaves for garnish

¼ teaspoon hot sauce

¼ teaspoon salt

1. Mash the avocado together with the, garlic, lemon juice, cilantro, hot sauce, and salt. Taste and add additional salt if desired.

Easy Hollandaise

YIELDS ABOUT 1 CUP, 8 (2-TABLESPOON) SERVINGS | PREP TIME: 10 MINUTES |
COOK TIME: N/A

10 tablespoons unsalted butter

3 large egg yolks

1 tablespoon fresh lemon juice

½ teaspoon Dijon mustard

¼ + ⅛ teaspoon salt

⅛ teaspoon black pepper

1. Melt the butter until hot in a microwave-safe bowl in the microwave or in a small saucepan on the stovetop. Don't let it boil; just cook until it's melted and hot.

2. Add the egg yolks, lemon juice, Dijon mustard, salt, and black pepper to a food processor and process until well-combined, about 1 minute, scraping down the sides as necessary.

3. Very slowly (starting with just 1 drop at a time), with the food processor running, drizzle the hot melted butter into the egg yolk mixture to temper. Continue this way until half of the butter is incorporated, and then add the remaining butter in a slow, steady drizzle with the food processor running.

4. You should end up with a smooth, emulsified sauce. If the sauce is too thick, you can drizzle water in (¼ teaspoon at a time) until it reaches the right consistency. Serve warm.

NOTE

- Hollandaise sauce is best served immediately once it's made. However, it can be made 1 day ahead and stored covered in the fridge. Reheat it in a double boiler until warm throughout.

Fresh Salsa

YIELDS ABOUT 10 (3-TABLESPOON) SERVINGS | PREP TIME: 10 MINUTES | COOK TIME: N/A

2 cups cherry tomatoes, quartered

½ medium-sized yellow or white onion, diced small

1 serrano pepper, minced

1 large clove garlic, minced

½ cup fresh chopped cilantro

1½ tablespoons fresh lime juice

¼ teaspoon salt

1. Stir together all ingredients in a large bowl.

2. Serve, or store covered in the fridge for up to 2 days.

NOTE

- If you can't find a serrano pepper, you can use jalapeño instead. Note that serrano peppers are quite a bit hotter than jalapeño peppers, so adjust accordingly.

About the Author

© Faith Gorsky

Faith Gorsky is a law-school-grad-turned-recipe-developer, food stylist, photographer, and published cookbook author. She authors the food blogs AnEdibleMosaic.com and HealthySweetEats.com, and coauthors TheKetoQueens.com. Faith is the author of *An Edible Mosaic: Middle Eastern Fare with Extraordinary Flair*, as well as the coauthor of *Keto Bread, The Keto Meal Plan Cookbook*, and *Keto Drinks*. Faith lives in St. Petersburg, Florida.

Conversion Charts

METRIC AND IMPERIAL CONVERSIONS

(These conversions are rounded for convenience)

Ingredient	Cups/ Tablespoons/ Teaspoons	Ounces	Grams/Milliliters
Butter	1 cup/ 16 tablespoons/ 2 sticks	8 ounces	230 grams
Cheese, shredded	1 cup	4 ounces	110 grams
Cream cheese	1 tablespoon	0.5 ounce	14.5 grams
Cornstarch	1 tablespoon	0.3 ounce	8 grams
Flour, all-purpose	1 cup/1 tablespoon	4.5 ounces/0.3 ounce	125 grams/8 grams
Flour, whole wheat	1 cup	4 ounces	120 grams
Fruit, dried	1 cup	4 ounces	120 grams
Fruits or veggies, chopped	1 cup	5 to 7 ounces	145 to 200 grams
Fruits or veggies, pureed	1 cup	8.5 ounces	245 grams
Honey, maple syrup, or corn syrup	1 tablespoon	0.75 ounce	20 grams
Liquids: cream, milk, water, or juice	1 cup	8 fluid ounces	240 milliliters
Oats	1 cup	5.5 ounces	150 grams
Salt	1 teaspoon	0.2 ounce	6 grams
Spices: cinnamon, cloves, ginger, or nutmeg (ground)	1 teaspoon	0.2 ounce	5 milliliters
Sugar, brown, firmly packed	1 cup	7 ounces	200 grams
Sugar, white	1 cup/1 tablespoon	7 ounces/0.5 ounce	200 grams/12.5 grams
Vanilla extract	1 teaspoon	0.2 ounce	4 grams

OVEN TEMPERATURES

Fahrenheit	Celsius	Gas Mark
225°	110°	¼
250°	120°	½
275°	140°	1
300°	150°	2
325°	160°	3
350°	180°	4
375°	190°	5
400°	200°	6
425°	220°	7
450°	230°	8

Recipe Index

Index

Notes

....

....

....

....

....

....

....

....

....

....

....

....

....

....

....

Notes

....

....

....

....

....

....

....

....

....

....

....

....

....

....

Notes

....

....

....

....

....

....

....

....

....

....

....

....

....

....

Notes

....

....

....

....

....

....

....

....

....

....

....

....

....

....

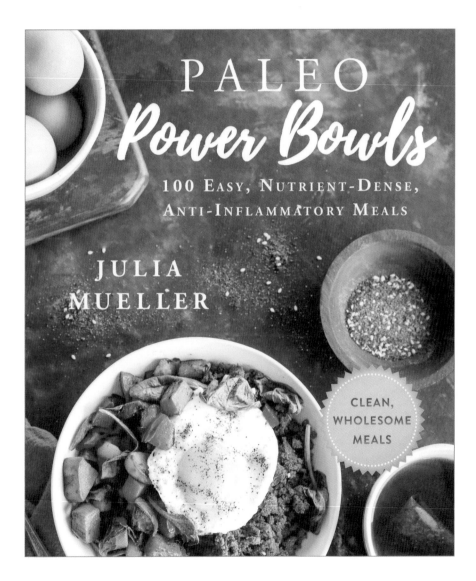

FOR MORE KETO TITLES

Fix-It and Forget-It
KETO COMFORT FOOD
Cookbook

127 SUPER EASY **SLOW COOKER** MEALS

HOPE COMERFORD

Fix-It and Forget-It®
Plant-Based
KETO
Cookbook

Low-Carb, Vegan Slow Cooker and Instant Pot Recipes

150 Healthy & Delicious Anti-Inflammatory Meals!

HOPE COMERFORD

Fix-It and Forget-It®
BIG BOOK OF
KETO RECIPES
275 HEALTHY **SLOW COOKER & INSTANT POT** FAVORITES

225 BONUS OVEN, STOVETOP, AND GRILLING RECIPES!

EDITED BY HOPE COMERFORD